# The MAILBOX®

# WONDER, DRAW, TELL!

## 77 storytelling opportunities for preschoolers

- Sparks curiosity and creativity
- Develops vocabulary and oral language
- Encourages communication skills
- Increases print awareness
- Supports popular teaching themes

*Capture the unique ideas of every child!*

**Managing Editor:** Kimberly Brugger-Murphy

**Editorial Team:** Becky S. Andrews, Diane Badden, Kimberley Bruck, Karen A. Brudnak, Pam Crane, Sarah Foreman, Pierce Foster, Tazmen Hansen, Marsha Heim, Lori Z. Henry, Debra Liverman, Kitty Lowrance, Brenda Miner, Jennifer Nunn, Mark Rainey, Greg D. Rieves, Hope Rodgers, Donna K. Teal, Rachael Traylor, Sharon M. Tresino

## www.themailbox.com

©2010 The Mailbox® Books
All rights reserved.
ISBN10 #1-56234-944-9 • ISBN13 #978-1-56234-944-8

Printed in the United States
10 9 8 7 6 5 4 3 2 1

HPS 215490

# Table of Contents

# What's Inside

**77 fun ways for little ones to wonder, draw, and tell!**

A label that shows the time of year and theme

A question that invites wonder

An illustration that encourages creative thinking

Space for a child to draw his or her ideas

Space for writing a child's dictation

## Cattail Critter

Spring
Pond life

**Wonder** What is peeking through the cattails?

**Draw**

**Tell**

by _____

*Wonder, Draw, Tell!* • ©The Mailbox® Books • TEC61273

# Up in the Tree

**Wonder** What happens next?

**Draw**

**Tell**

by _____

# Munch and Crunch

**Wonder** Who ate the apple?

**Draw**

**Tell**

by _____

# Tasty Apple Treats

**Wonder** What gets made with these apples?

**Draw**

**Tell**

by _____

*Wonder, Draw, Tell!* • ©The Mailbox® Books • TEC61273

# Lurking in the Leaves

**Wonder** What is in the leaf pile?

**Draw**

**Tell**

by _____

# Get That Leaf!

**Wonder** What is chasing the leaf?

**Draw**

**Tell**

**by** _____

*Wonder, Draw, Tell!* • ©The Mailbox® Books • TEC61273

## Fun With Bear

**Wonder** What is Bear doing with the leaves?

**Draw**

**Tell**

*Wonder, Draw, Tell!* • ©The Mailbox® Books • TEC61273

# Nighttime Visitors

**Wonder** What visits the pumpkin patch at night?

**Draw**

**Tell**

by _____

# One Big Pumpkin!

**Wonder** Where is Turkey taking the pumpkin?

**Draw**

**Tell**

by _____

# Hide-and-Seek

**Wonder** What is hiding in the pumpkin?

**Draw**

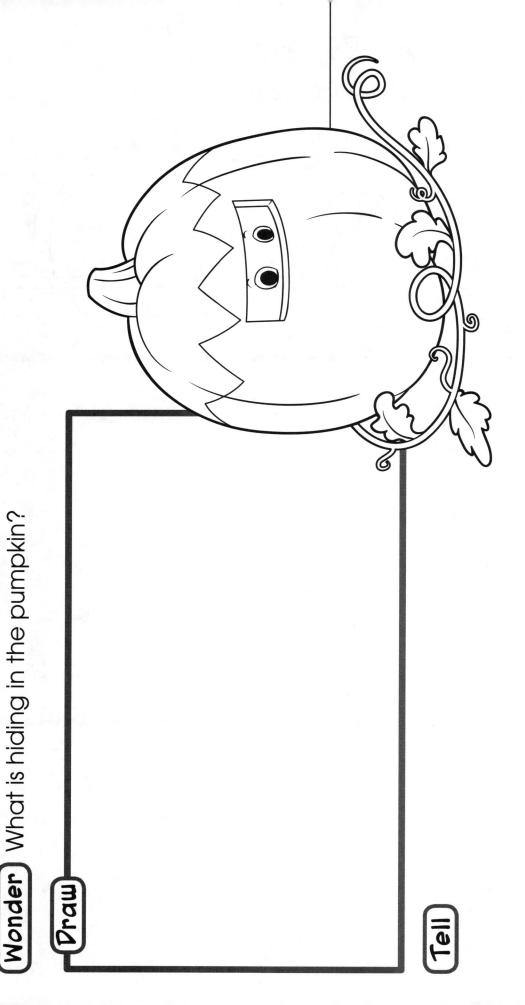

**Tell**

by _____

# On a Roll

Wonder   What will happen next?

Draw

Tell

by _____

# Dinner Guest

**Wonder** Who is coming to Thanksgiving dinner?

**Draw**

**Tell**

by _____

# Time to Hide!

**Wonder** Where do turkeys hide on Thanksgiving?

**Draw**

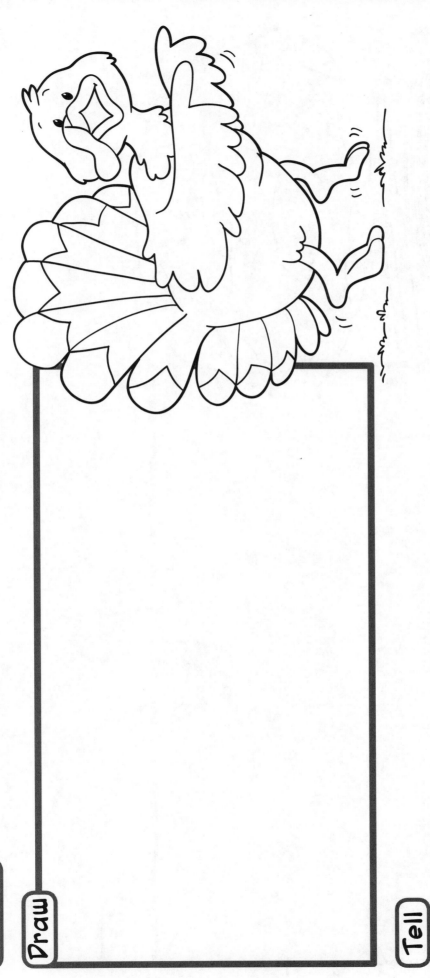

**Tell**

by _____

*Wonder, Draw, Tell!* • ©The Mailbox® Books • TEC61273

# Pleasing Pie

**Wonder** Who is going to eat this pie?

**Draw**

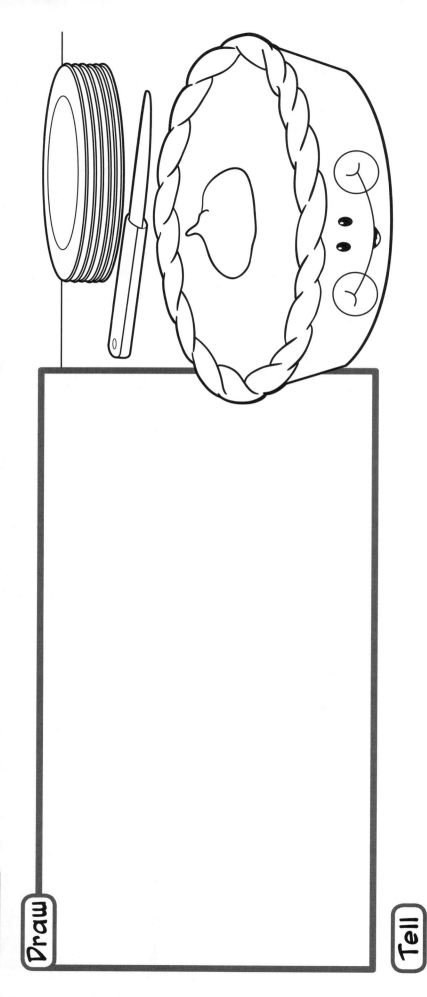

**Tell**

by _____

16

# Santa's Workshop

**Wonder** What is the elf going to make?

**Draw**

**Tell**

by _____

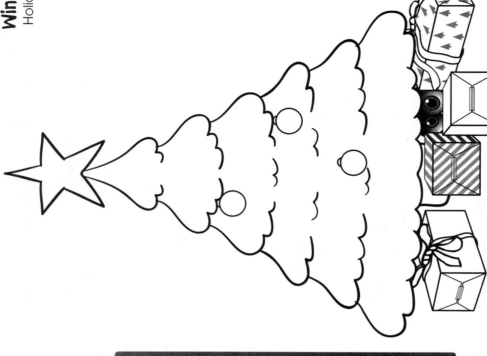

# Cozy Tree

**Wonder** What is under the Christmas tree?

**Draw**

**Tell**

by

# Missing Cookies

**Wonder** Where are Santa's cookies?

**Draw**

**Tell**

**by** _____

# A Gift for Santa

**Wonder** What would you put in Santa's stocking?

**Draw**

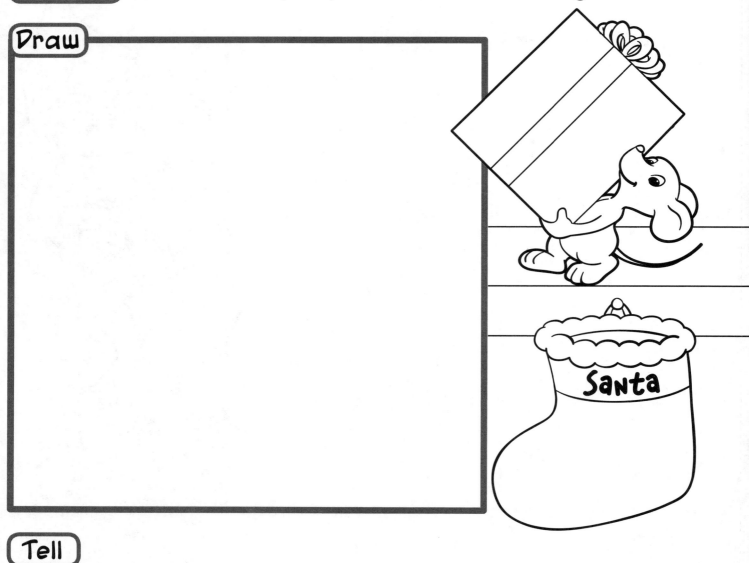

**Tell**

**by** _____

## Hanukkah Gift

**Wonder**  What is in the box?

**Draw**

**Tell**

by _____

*Wonder, Draw, Tell!* • ©The Mailbox® Books • TEC61273

# Harvest Fruits

Wonder What kind of fruit is in the bowl?

Draw

Tell

*Wonder, Draw, Tell!* • ©The Mailbox® Books • TEC61273

by

# Clever Penguin

**Wonder** What is Penguin going to do?

**Draw**

**Tell**

by _____

# So Many Snowballs!

**Wonder** What happens next?

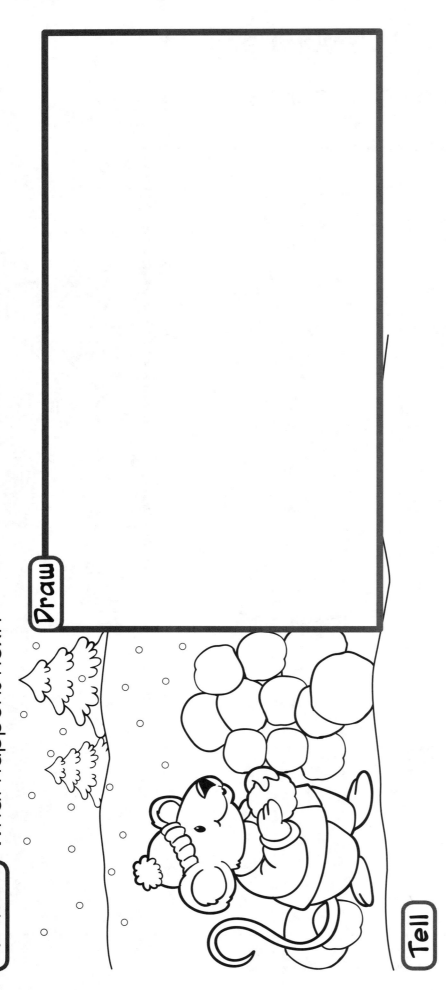

**Draw**

**Tell**

by _____

*Wonder, Draw, Tell!* • ©The Mailbox® Books • TEC61273

# Cozy Winter Hat

**Wonder** What is sleeping under the hat?

**Draw**

**Tell**

by _____

# Snow Buddies

**Wonder** Who is coming to play with Bear?

**Draw**

**Tell**

**by** _____

 *Wonder, Draw, Tell!* • ©The Mailbox® Books • TEC61273

# Hidden Surprise

**Wonder** What is Dog hiding?

**Draw**

**Tell**

**by** _____

## Someone Special

**Wonder** Who gave Kitty a card?

**Draw**

**Tell**

by _____

_Wonder, Draw, Tell!_ • ©The Mailbox® Books • TEC61273

# Candy Caper

**Wonder** What happened to the candy?

**Draw**

**Tell**

by _____

# Bunch of Balloons

**Wonder** What happens next?

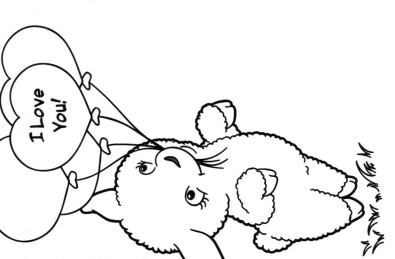

**Draw**

**Tell**

by _____

# Phone a Friend

**Wonder** Who is Squirrel talking to?

**Draw**

**Tell**

**by** _____

32

# Best of Friends

**Wonder** Who is coming to play with Turtle?

**Draw**

TOYS

**Tell**

by _____

# Puddle Play

**Wonder** What is playing in the puddles?

**Draw**

**Tell**

by _____

_Wonder, Draw, Tell!_ • ©The Mailbox® Books • TEC61273

# Sunny-Day Fun

**Wonder** What do you like to do on a sunny day?

**Draw**

**Tell**

**by** _____

# A Windy Day!

**Wonder** Where will Mouse land?

**Draw**

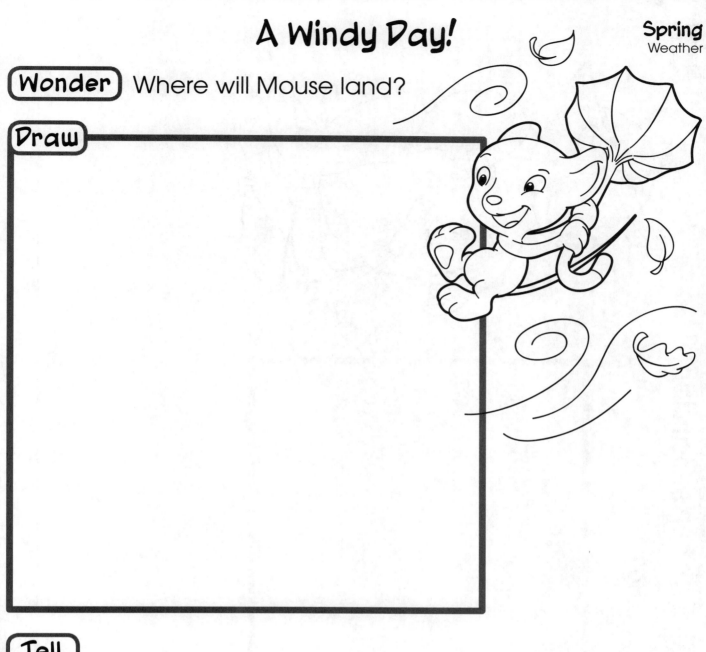

**Tell**

by _____

# Gopher's Garden

**Wonder** What is Gopher growing?

**Draw**

**Tell**

by _____

# Planting Possibilities

**Wonder** What would you plant in a garden?

**Draw**

**Tell**

**by** _____

# Skunk's Surprise

**Wonder** What is in Skunk's garden?

**Draw**

**Tell**

by _____

# Dinnertime!

**Wonder** What will you make with the vegetables?

**Draw**

**Tell**

by _____

shhhhhh

# An "Egg-cellent" Trip

**Wonder** Where is Bunny taking the eggs?

**Draw**

**Tell**

by _____

*Wonder, Draw, Tell!* • ©The Mailbox® Books • TEC61273

# Rain, Rain, Go Away!

**Wonder** What should Bunny do on a rainy day?

**Draw**

**Tell**

**by** _____

# Bunny's Bag

Wonder  Why did Bunny go to the store?

Draw

Tell

by _____

# Cattail Critter

**Wonder** What is peeking through the cattails?

**Draw**

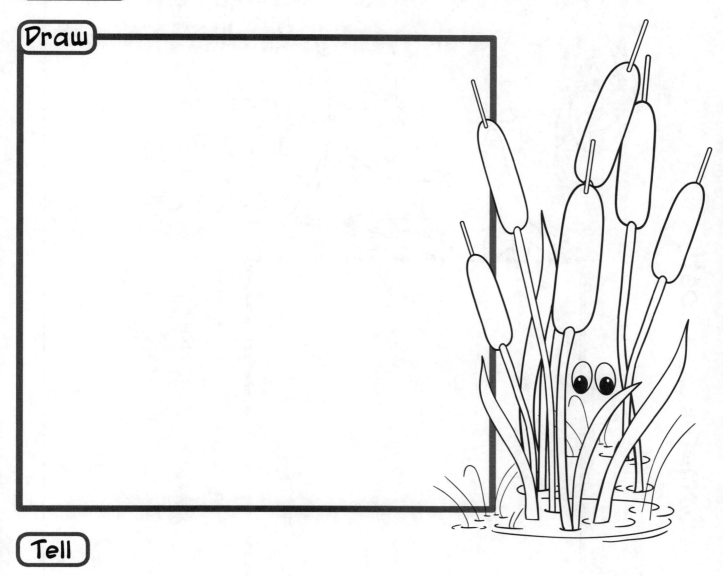

**Tell**

by _____

# Something Is Lost!

**Wonder** What is Duck looking for?

**Draw**

**Tell**

by _____

*Wonder, Draw, Tell!* • ©The Mailbox® Books • TEC61273

# Hop, Hop, Hop!

**Wonder** Why is Frog hopping?

**Draw**

**Tell**

by _____

_Wonder, Draw, Tell!_ • ©The Mailbox® Books • TEC61273

# A Turtle Tale

**Wonder** What are the turtles waiting for?

**Draw**

**Tell**

by _____

46

# Beautiful Colors

**Wonder** What is Butterfly painting?

**Draw**

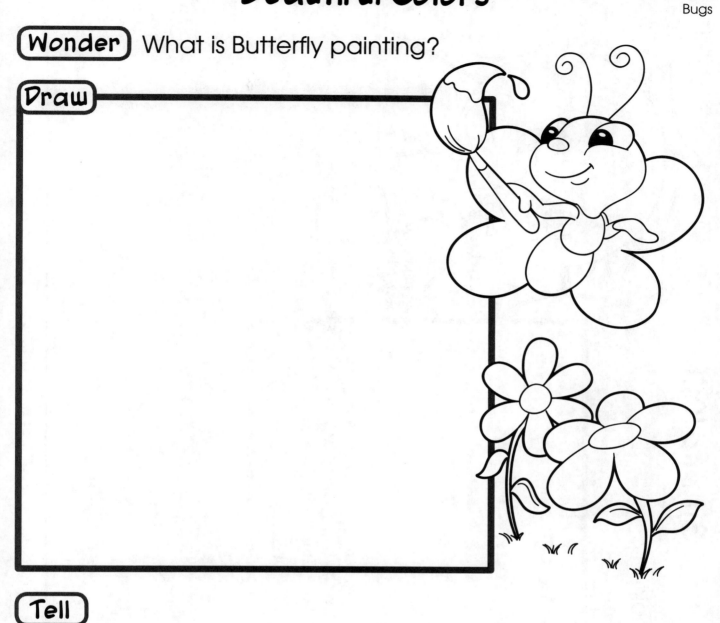

**Tell**

by _____

# Sit and Knit

**Wonder** What is Spider making?

**Draw**

**Tell**

by _____

*Wonder, Draw, Tell!* ©The Mailbox® Books • TEC61273

# Buzz, Buzz, Buzz

**Wonder** Where is Bee going?

**Draw**

**Tell**

by _____

# Naptime!

**Wonder** What is Ladybug dreaming about?

**Draw**

**Tell**

by _____

# Comfy Castle

**Wonder** Who lives in this sand castle?

**Draw**

**Tell**

by _____

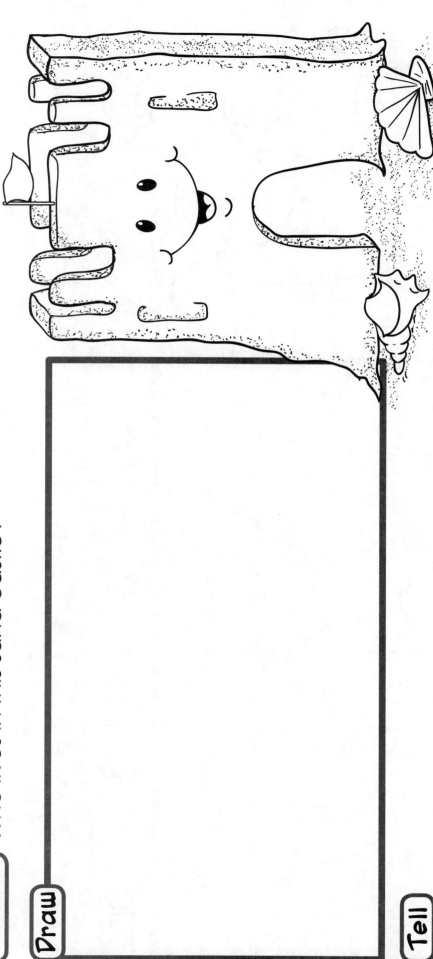

# Starfish Friends

**Wonder** Who is Starfish playing with?

**Draw**

**Tell**

by

*Wonder, Draw, Tell!* • ©The Mailbox® Books • TEC61273

# Creative Crab

**Wonder** Why did Crab dig a hole?

**Draw**

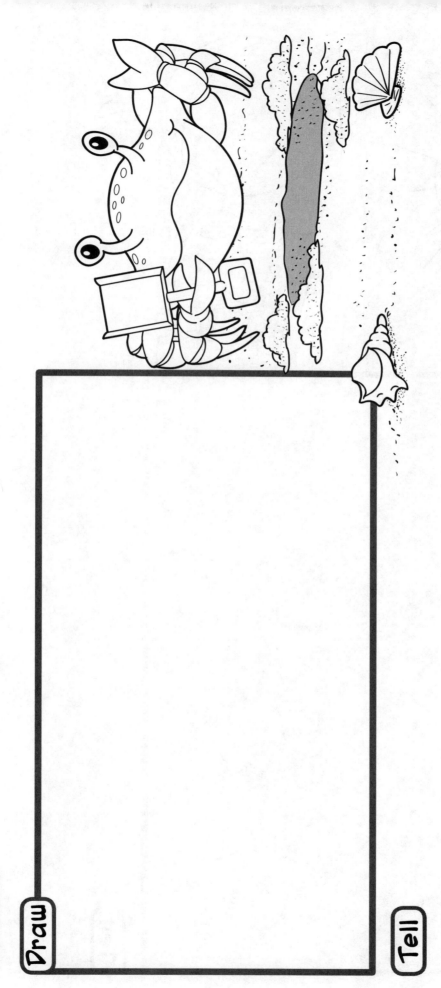

**Tell**

# Beach Fun!

**Wonder** What would you do at the beach?

**Draw**

**Tell**

by _____

*Wonder, Draw, Tell!* • ©The Mailbox® Books • TEC61273

# Picnic Surprise!

**Wonder** What is in the picnic basket?

**Draw**

**Tell**

by _____

# Humongous Melon

**Wonder** What happens next?

**Draw**

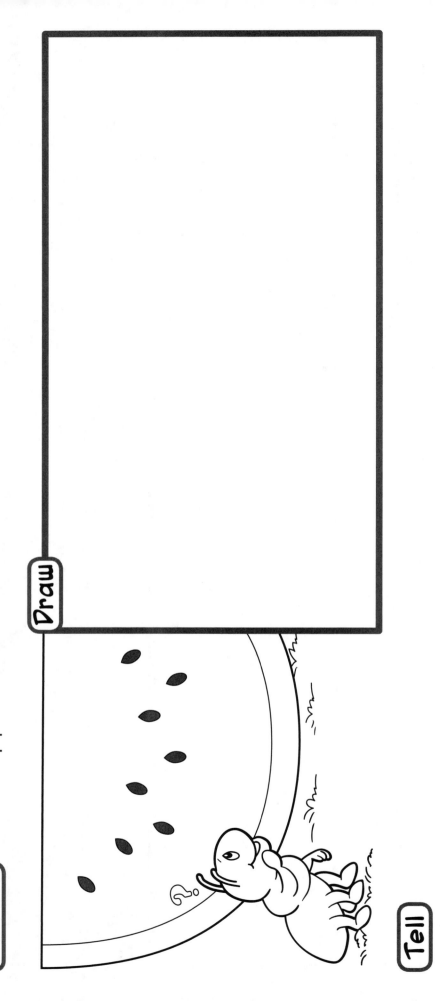

**Tell**

by _____

_Wonder, Draw, Tell!_ • ©The Mailbox® Books • TEC61273

# Craving Cake

**Wonder** Who will eat the cake?

**Draw**

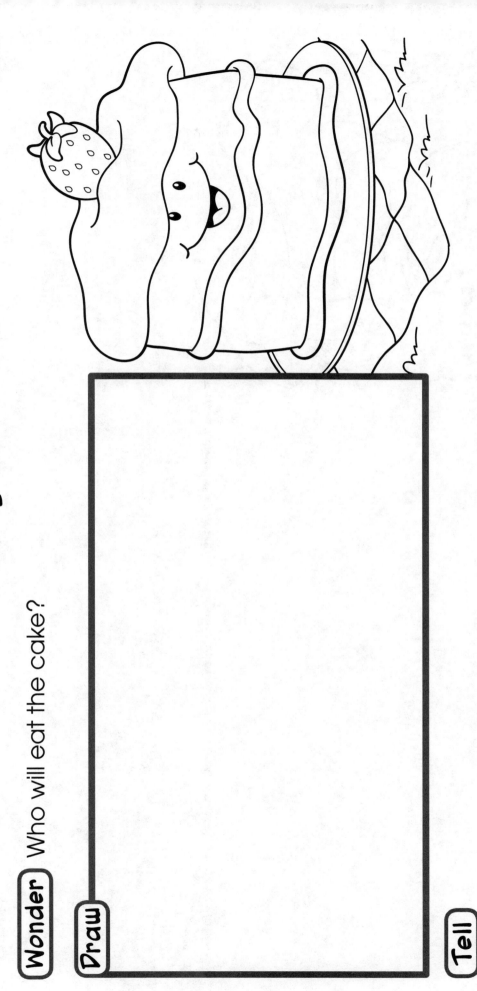

**Tell**

by _____

*Wonder, Draw, Tell!* • ©The Mailbox® Books • TEC61273

# All Gone!

**Wonder** Who ate all of Bear's ice cream?

**Draw**

**Tell**

by _____

_Wonder, Draw, Tell!_ • ©The Mailbox® Books • TEC61273

# Ice Cream Options

**Wonder** Which flavor is Flamingo's favorite?

**Draw**

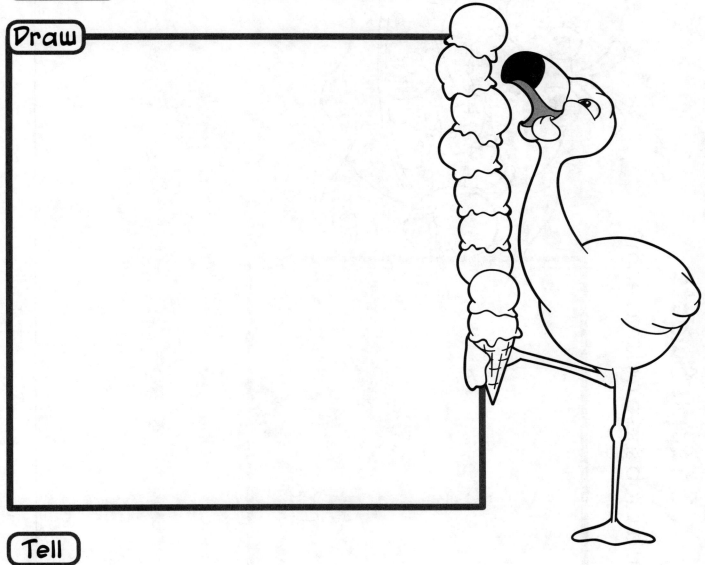

**Tell**

by _____

# Snappy Sweets

**Wonder** With whom should Crab share his ice cream?

**Draw**

**Tell**

by _____

# On the Way!

**Wonder** Where is the fire truck going?

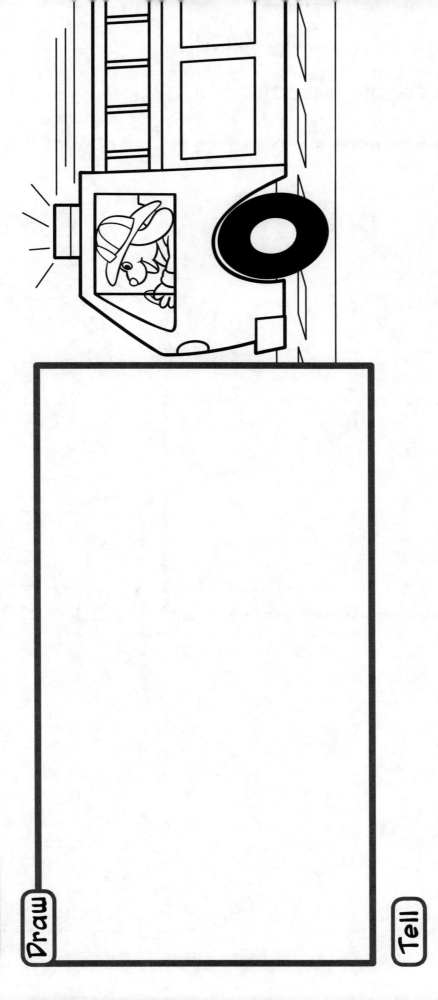

**Draw**

**Tell**

by _____

# Say Aah!

**Wonder** What is in the doctor's bag?

**Draw**

**Tell**

**by** _____

# Something Smells Yummy!

**Wonder** What is the chef cooking?

**Draw**

**Tell**

by _____

# "Dino-mite" Dinosaur

**Wonder** How could Dinosaur be helpful?

**Draw**

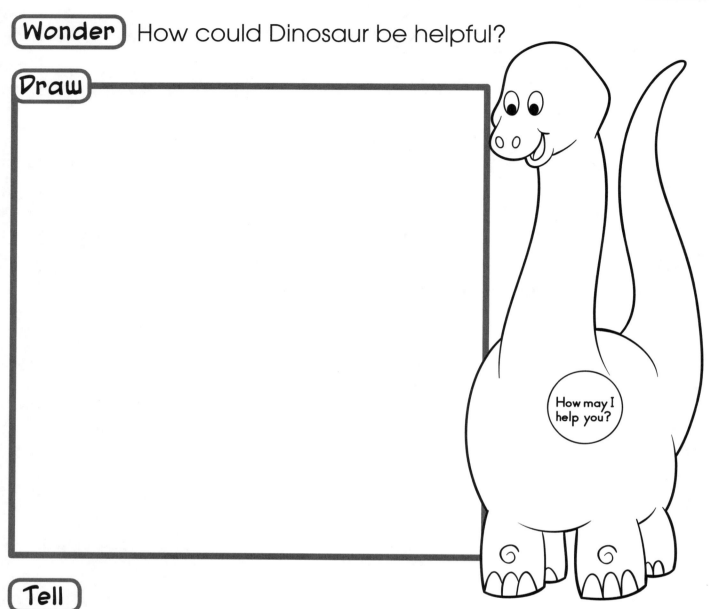

How may I help you?

**Tell**

**by** _____

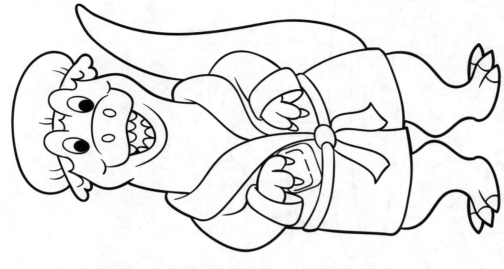

# Squeaky Clean

**Wonder** Where will Dinosaur take a bath?

**Draw**

**Tell**

by

*Wonder, Draw, Tell!* • ©The Mailbox® Books • TEC61273

# Breakfast Time!

**Wonder** What will Dinosaur eat for breakfast?

**Draw**

**Tell**

by _____

# Farmer's Busy Day

**Wonder** Why does the farmer have a pail?

**Draw**

**Tell**

by _____

# Peekaboo Barn

**Wonder** What is peeking out of the barn?

**Draw**

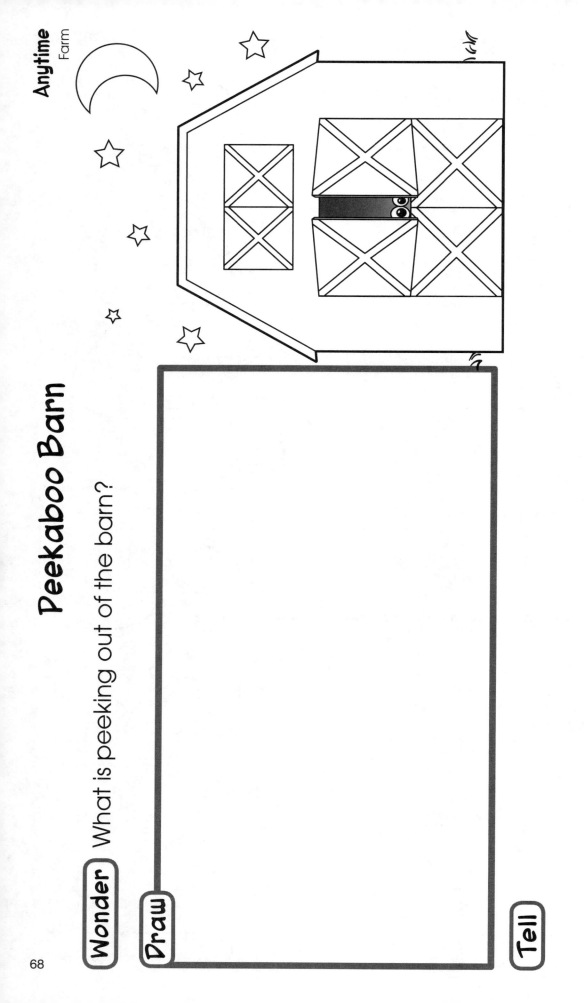

**Tell**

by _____

# Bye-Bye, Pig

**Wonder** Where is Pig going?

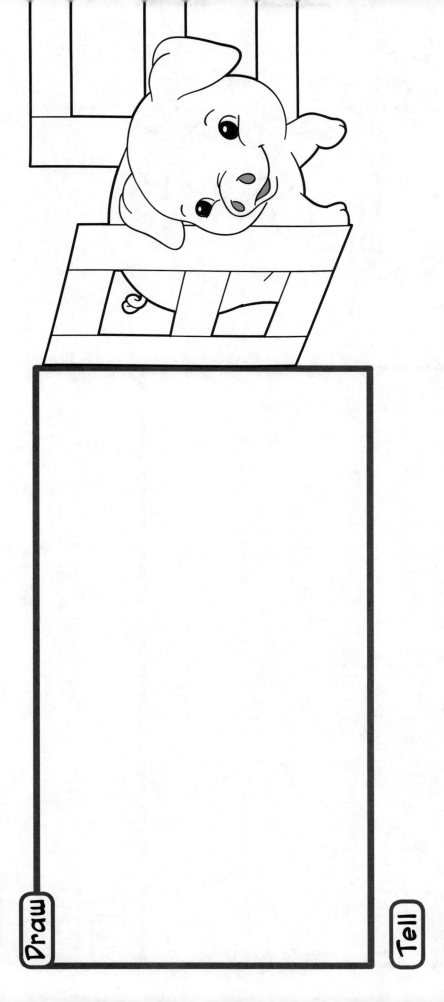

**Draw**

**Tell**

by _____

*Wonder, Draw, Tell!* • ©The Mailbox® Books • TEC61273

# Chicks on the Move

**Wonder** Why are the chicks running?

**Draw**

**Tell**

by

# Go, Max, Go!

**Wonder** Why is Max running?

**Draw**

**Tell**

by _____

# Swinging and Singing

**Wonder** What happens next?

**Draw**

**Tell**

by _____

_Wonder, Draw, Tell!_ • ©The Mailbox® Books • TEC61273

# Playful Kitty

**Wonder** What does Kitty like to do?

**Draw**

**Tell**

by _____

# Time to Fly!

**Wonder** Where is the plane going?

**Draw**

**Tell**

by _____

*Wonder, Draw, Tell!* ©The Mailbox® Books • TEC61273

# Biking Buddies

**Wonder** Who is riding bikes with Monkey?

**Draw**

**Tell**

by _____

*Wonder, Draw, Tell!* • ©The Mailbox® Books • TEC61273

# Stormy Day

**Wonder**  What happens next?

**Draw**

**Tell**

by _____

# Take a Trip!

**Wonder**  Where is your favorite place to go?

**Draw**

**Tell**

# At the Zoo

**Wonder** What is the zookeeper's favorite job?

**Draw**

**Tell**

by _____

*Wonder, Draw, Tell!* • ©The Mailbox® Books • TEC61273

# Tiger Time

**Wonder** What do tigers like to do?

**Draw**

**Tell**

by _____

# Sightseeing

Wonder  What animals would you like to see?

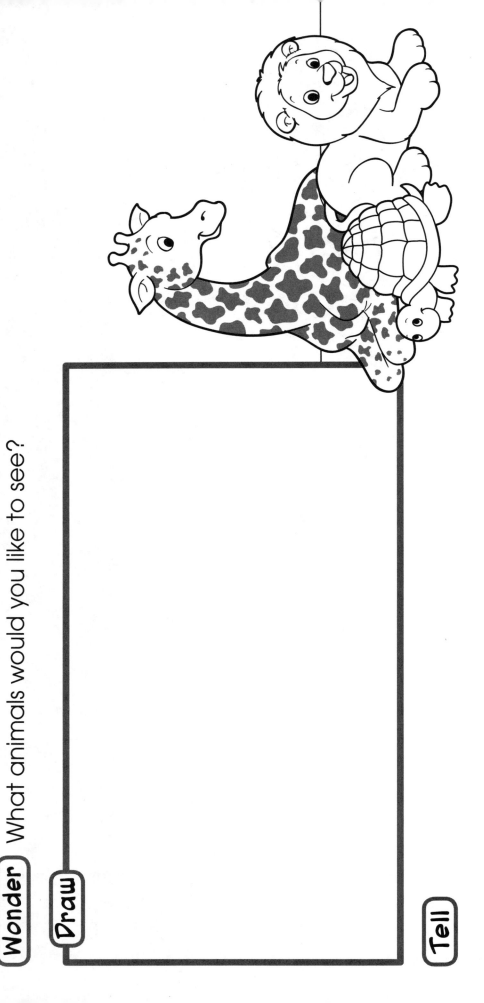

Draw

Tell

by _____

*Wonder, Draw, Tell!* • ©The Mailbox® Books • TEC61273